PUNCH LIBRARY OF HUMOUR

Edited by J. A. HAMMERTON

❧ Designed to provide in a series of volumes, each complete in itself, the cream of our national humour, contributed by the masters of comic draughtsmanship and the leading wits of the age to "Punch," from its beginning in 1841 to the present day ❧ ❧ ❧ ❧

MR. PUNCH AT THE PLAY

Actor (on the stage). " Me mind is made up ! "
Voice from the Gallery. " What abeaout yer fice ? "

MR. PUNCH
AT THE PLAY

HUMOURS OF MUSIC AND
THE DRAMA

WITH 140 ILLUSTRATIONS

BY

CHARLES KEENE, PHIL
MAY, GEORGE DU MAU-
RIER, BERNARD PART-
RIDGE, L. RAVEN-HILL,
E. T. REED, F. H. TOWN-
SEND, C. E. BROCK, A. S.
BOYD, TOM BROWNE,
EVERARD HOP-
KINS AND
OTHERS

PUBLISHED BY SPECIAL ARRANGEMENT WITH

THE PROPRIETORS OF "PUNCH"

🍃 🍃 🍃

THE EDUCATIONAL BOOK CO. LTD.

THE PUNCH LIBRARY OF HUMOUR

Twenty-five volumes, crown 8vo, 192 pages
fully illustrated

LIFE IN LONDON
COUNTRY LIFE
IN THE HIGHLANDS
SCOTTISH HUMOUR
IRISH HUMOUR
COCKNEY HUMOUR
IN SOCIETY
AFTER DINNER STORIES
IN BOHEMIA
AT THE PLAY
MR. PUNCH AT HOME
ON THE CONTINONG

RAILWAY BOOK
AT THE SEASIDE
MR. PUNCH AFLOAT
IN THE HUNTING FIELD
MR. PUNCH ON TOUR
WITH ROD AND GUN
MR. PUNCH AWHEEL
BOOK OF SPORTS
GOLF STORIES
IN WIG AND GOWN
ON THE WARPATH
BOOK OF LOVE

WITH THE CHILDREN

BEFORE THE CURTAIN

MOST of the PUNCH artists of note have used their pencils on the theatre; with theatricals public and private none has done more than Du Maurier. All have made merry over the extravagances of melodrama and "problem" plays; the vanity and the mistakes of actors, actresses and dramatists; and the blunderings of the average playgoer.

MR. PUNCH genially satirises the aristocratic amateurs who, some few years ago, made frantic rushes into the profession, and for a while enjoyed more kudos as actors than they had obtained as titled members of the upper circle, and the exaggerated social status that for the time accrued to the professional actor as a consequence of this invasion.

The things he has written about the stage, quite apart from all reviewing of plays, would more than fill a book of itself; and he has slyly and laughingly satirised players, playwrights and public with an equal impartiality.

He has got a deal of fun out of the French dramas and the affected pleasure taken in them by audiences that did not understand the language. He has got even more fun out of the dramatists whose " original plays " were largely translated from the French, and to whom Paris was, and to some extent is still, literally and figuratively "a playground."

MR. PUNCH
AT THE PLAY

SOMETHING FOR THE MONEY

(From the Playgoers' Conversation Book.   Coming Edition.)

I HAVE only paid three guineas and a half for this stall, but it is certainly stuffed with the very best hair.

The people in the ten - and - sixpenny gallery seem fairly pleased with their dado.

I did not know the call-boy was at Eton.

The expenses of this house must be enormous, if they always play *Box and Cox* with a rasher of real Canadian bacon.

How nice to know that the musicians, though out of sight under the stage, are in evening dress on velvet cushions !

7

Whoever is the author of this comedy, he has not written up with spirit to that delightful Louis the Fifteenth linen cupboard.

I cannot catch a word "Macbeth" is saying, but I can see at a glance that his kilt would be extremely cheap at seventy pounds.

I am not surprised to hear that the "Tartar's lips" for the cauldron alone add nightly something like fifty-five-and-sixpence to the expenses.

Do not bother me about the situation when I am looking at the quality of the velvet pile.

Since the introduction of the *live* hedgehog into domestic drama obliged the management to raise the second-tier private boxes to forty guineas, the Duchess has gone into the slips with an order.

They had, perhaps, better take away the champagne-bottle and the diamond-studded whistle from the prompter.

Ha! here comes the chorus of villagers, provided with real silk pocket-handkerchiefs.

It is all this sort of thing that elevates the drama, and makes me so contented to part with a ten-pound note for an evening's amusement.

Pantomime Child (to admiring friend). "Yus, and there's another hadvantage in bein' a hactress. You get yer fortygraphs took for noffink!"

THE HEIGHT OF LITERARY NECESSITY.—
"Spouting" Shakspeare.

WHEN are parsons bound in honour not to
abuse theatres?

When they take orders.

WHAT VOTE THE MANAGER OF A THEATRE
ALWAYS HAS.—The "casting" vote.

"STAND NOT ON THE ORDER OF YOUR GOING."
—An amiable manager says the orders which he
issues for the pit and gallery are what in his
opinion constitute "the lower orders."

GREAT THEATRICAL EFFECT.—During a performance of *Macbeth* at the Haymarket, the
thunder was so natural that it turned sour a pint
of beer in the prompter's-box.

THE DRAMA.—"''Ere, I say, 'Liza, we've seen this 'ere play before!"   "No, we ain't."   [*Wordy argument follows.*]   "Why, don't you remember, same time as Bill took us to the 'Pig an' Whistle,' an' we 'ad stewed eels for supper?"   "Oh lor! Yes, that takes me back to it!"

TRUE APPRECIATION

(*Overheard at the Theatre*)

Mrs. Parvenu. "I don't know that I'm exackly *gone* on Shakspeare
Plays." [*Mr. P. agrees.*

12

Conversationalist. "Do you play ping-pong?"
Actor. "No. I play *Hamlet!*"

13

To Actors who are not worth a Thought.
—We notice that there is a book called "Acting and Thinking." This is to distinguish it, we imagine, from the generality of acting, in which there is mostly no thinking ?

A Crusher.—*Country Manager (to Mr. Agrippa Snap, the great London critic, who has come down to see the production of a piece on trial).* And what do you think, sir, of our theatre and our players ?

Agrippa Snap (loftily). Well, frankly, Mr. Flatson, your green-room's better than your company.

The higher walk of the drama.

"Auntie, can *you* do that?"

15

THEATRICAL managers are so often accused of being unable to break with tradition, that it seems only fair to point out that several of them have recently produced plays, in which the character of "Hamlet" does not appear at all.

ON A DRAMATIC AUTHOR

"YES, he's a plagiarist," from Tom this fell,
  "As to his social faults, sir, one excuses 'em;
'Cos he's good natured, takes a joke so well."
  "True," cries an author, "He takes mine and uses 'em."

THE MANAGER'S COMPLAINT

SHE danced among the unfinished ways
  That merge into the Strand,
A maid whom none could fail to praise,
  And very few withstand.

A sylph, accepted for the run,
  Not at a weekly wage;
Fair as a star when only one
  Is shining on the stage.

She met a lord, and all men know
  How soon she'd done with me;
Now she is in *Debrett*, oh, and,
  That's where they all would be!

A FIRST NIGHT.—*Indignant Playwright (to leading actor, behind the scenes).* "Confound it, man, you've absolutely murdered the piece!" *Leading Actor.* "Pardon me, but I think the foul play is yours!"

Smart. How do, Smooth? (*to theatrical manager, who frowns upon him*). What's the matter, eh?

Smooth. Matter? Hang it, Smart, you wrote me down in "The Stinger."

Smart (*repressing something Shakspearian about "writing down" which occurs to him, continues pleasantly*). Wrote you down? No, I said the piece was a bad one, because I thought it was; a very bad one.

Smooth. Bad! (*Sarcastically.*) You were the only man who said so.

Smart (*very pleasantly*). My dear fellow, *I was the only man who saw it.* Good-bye.

[*Exeunt severally.*

MOTTO FOR A BOX-OFFICE KEEPER.—" So much for booking 'em."

"A CONSIDERABLE demonstration of approval greeted the fall of the curtain." How are we to take this?

18

"THE DESIRE OF THE MOTH FOR THE STAR."—*Mistress.* "And you dare to tell me, Belinda, that you have actually answered a *theatrical advertisement*? How *could* you be such *a wicked girl*?" *Belinda* (*whimpering*). "Well, mum,—*other young lidies*—gow on the—stige—why shouldn't I gow?"

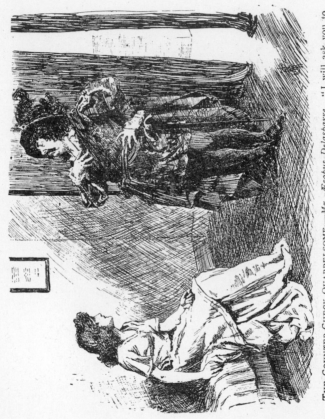

THE COUNTER-CHECK QUARRELSOME.—*Mr. Æsopus Delasparre.* "I will ask you to favour me, madam, by refraining from laughing at me on the stage during my third act." *Miss Jowls (sweetly).* "Oh, but I assure you you're mistaken, Mr. Delasparre; I never laugh at you on the stage—I wait till I get home!"

SWEEPING ASSERTION.—"The other night, at the Novelty Theatre, Mrs. Vere-Jones was gowned simply in a *clinging* black velvet, with a cloak of same handsomely trimmed with ermine."—*Extract from Society Journal.*

DRAMATIC NOTES OF THE FUTURE

[A little cheild is the hero of *Everybody's Secret;* the curtain rises upon four little cheildren in *Her Own Way;* there are cheildren of various ages in *Alice-Sit-by-the-fire.*]

Mr. Barrie's new play, *The Admirable Crèche,* will be presented to-morrow. We understand that there is a pretty scene in the third act in which several grown-ups are discovered smoking cigars. It may confidently be predicted that all the world will rush to the " Duke of York's " to see this novelty. *The Admirable Crèche* will be preceded at 8.30 by *Bassinette—A Plea for a Numerous Family,* a one-act play by Theodore Roosevelt and Louis N. Parker.

Little Baby Wilkins is making quite a name with her wonderful rendering of " Perdita " in the Haymarket version of *A Winter's Tale.* As soon as actor-manager Wilkins realised the necessity of cutting the last two acts (in which " Perdita " is grown up) the play was bound to succeed. By the

MODERN IMPRESSIONIST ART. A MUSICAL COMEDY

way, Mr. E. H. Cooper's new book, " Perditas 1 have Known," is announced.

Frankly, we are disappointed in Mr. Pinero's new play, *Little Arthur*, produced at Wyndham's last week. It treated of the old old theme—the love of the hero for his nurse. To be quite plain, this stale triangle, mother—son—nurse, is beginning to bore us. Are there no other themes in every-day life which Mr. Pinero might take? Could he not, for instance, give us an analysis ot the mind of a young genius torn between the necessity for teething and the desire to edit a great daily? Duty calls him both ways: his duty to himself and his duty to the public. Imagine a Wilkins in such a scene!

The popular editor of the " Nursery," whose unrivalled knowledge of children causes him to be referred to everywhere as our greatest playwright, is a little at sea in his latest play, *Rattles*. In the first act he rashly introduces (though by this time he should know his own limitations) two grown-ups at lunch—Mr. Jones the father, and Dr. Brown, who discuss Johnny's cough. Now we would point out to Mr. Crouper that men of their

24

AT THE PREMIÈRE

Lady in Front Row (to her neighbour, towards the end of the second act). " Who is this man next me, who's just come in,—do you know ? He doesn't seem to be paying the smallest attention to the play ! "

Her Neighbour. " Oh, I expect he's a critic. He's probably made up his mind long ago what he's going to say of the piece ; but he's just dropped in to *confirm his suspicions.*"

25

age would be unlikely to have milk for lunch ; and that they would not say " Yeth, pleath "—unless of Hebraic origin, and Mr. Crouper does not say so anywhere. Mr. Crouper must try and see something of grown-ups before he writes a play of this kind again.

We regret to announce that Cecil Tomkins, *doyen* of actor-managers, is down again with mumps.

No First-Nighter.—*First Man in the Street.* See the eclipse last night ?

Second Man in the Street. No. Thought it might be crowded. Put off going till next week.

THE BILL OF THE PLAY.

AMENITIES OF THE PROFESSION.—*Rising Young Drama-*
tist. " Saw your wife in front last night. What did she
think of my new comedy ? "   *Brother Playwright.*   " Oh,
I think she liked it. She told me she had a good laugh."
R. Y. D.   " Ah—er—when was that ? "   *B. P.*   " During
the *entr'acte*. One of the attendants dropped an ice down
her neighbour's neck."

27

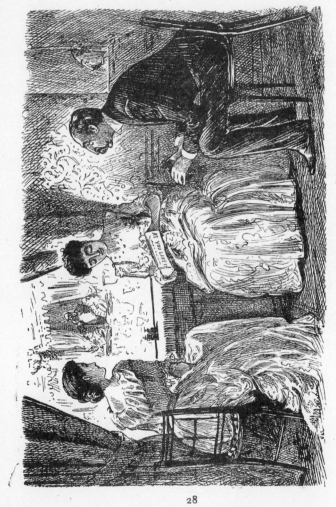

THE HIGHER EDUCATION OF WOMEN

Dora (consulting a playbill). "Only fancy! '*As You Like It*' is by Shakspeare!"

PRIVATE THEATRICALS. A REHEARSAL.—*The Captain.* "At this stage of the proceedings I've got to kiss you, Lady Grace. Will your husband mind, do you think?" *Lady Grace.* "Oh no! It's for a *charity*, you know!"

AN INFANT ROSCIUS.—*Stage Manager (interviewing children with the idea of engaging them for a new play).* "Has this child been on the stage?" *Proud Mother.* "No; but he's been on an inquest, and he speaks up fine!"

A SOLILOQUY.—*Tragedian.* "Cheap. Ha, ha! Why in my time they *threw* them at us!"

"Well, papa, how did you enjoy the play to-night?"
"Oh, I think I enjoyed it fairly well, my dear. I've got
a general sort of idea that I didn't go to sleep over it!"

Enthusiastic Lady Amateur. "Oh, what a pity! We've just missed the first act!" *Languid Friend.* "Have we? Ah—rather glad. I always think the chief pleasure of going to a theatre is trying to make out what the first act was about!"

THEATRICAL.—When it is announced that an actor will be supported by the *entire* company, it is not thereby meant that the said professional is sustained in his arduous part solely by draughts of Barclay, Perkins and Co.

THE wretch who refuses to take his wife to the theatre deserves to be made to sit out a play.

GOOD "PIECE" OF FURNITURE FOR THEATRICAL MANAGERS.—A chest of "drawers."

REGENERATION OF THE BRITISH DRAMA.—There are at this moment three English managers in Paris "in search of novelty!" More: three distinguished members of the Dramatic Authors' Society started for France last night.

"AS GOOD AS A PLAY."—Performing a funeral.

A PLANT IN SEASON.—Now is the time of year when managers of theatres show a botanical taste, for there is not one of them who does not do his best to have a great rush at his doors.

THE DRAMATIC AUTHOR'S PLAYGROUND.—Paris.

THEATRICAL NOTE.—*Net* profits are generally the result of a good "*cast.*"

"Shakspeare and the first Quart O"

A DUBIOUS COMPLIMENT. — *Rector's Wife* (*after harvest festival*). Well, Mrs. Piggleswade, how did you like the Bishop's sermon?

Mrs. Piggleswade. Oh! ma'am, I ain't been so much upset since my old man took me to the wariety theayter in London last August twelvemonth, and 'eard a gen'leman sing about his grandmother's cat.

" Shakspeare and the last Quart O "

THERE was a poor actor on the Norwich circuit
who squinted most dreadfully : he was put up on
one occasion for " Lear." " We must succeed," said
the manager, " for there never was a *Lear* with so
strong a *cast*."

A RICHMOND DINNER.—A shouting actor who
performs the part.

BY DEPUTY

As Shakspeare could not write his plays
   (If Mrs. Gallup's not mistaken),
I think how wise in many ways
   He was to have them done by Bacon;
They might have mouldered on the shelf,
   Mere minor dramas (and he knew it!)
If he had written them himself
   Instead of letting Bacon do it.

And if it's true, as Brown and Smith
   In many learned tomes have stated,
That Homer was an idle myth,
   He ought to be congratulated;
Since, thus evading birth, he rose
   For men to worship from a distance:
He might have penned inferior prose
   Had he achieved a real existence.

To him and Shakspeare some agree
   In making very nice allusions,
But no one thinks of praising me,
   For I composed my own effusions:
As others wrote their works divine,
   And they immortal thus to day are,
If someone else had written mine
   I might have been as great as they are!

Famous Lion Comique (to his agent, who is not much of a cigar smoker). "What did you think of that cigar as I give you the other day?" *Agent.* "Well, the first night I liked it well enough. But the second night I didn't like it so well. And the third I didn't like it at all!"

39

NUMEROUS applications were received by the manager of Covent Garden from "professionals" wishing to take part in *The Forty Thieves*. It was not found possible to offer engagements to the following (amongst others) :—

The Thief—who stole a march.

The Thief—in the candle.

The Thief—who was set to catch a thief.

The Thief—who stole the "purse" and found it "trash."

The Thief—who stole up-stairs.

The Thief—of time, *alias* procrastination, and—

The Thief—who stole a kiss (overwhelming number of applicants).

THE REAL AND THE IDEAL; OR, THE CATAS-
TROPHE OF A VICTORIA MELO-DRAMA

Berthelda.—Sanguino, you have killed your *mother ! ! !*

Fruitwoman.—Any apples, oranges, biscuits, ginger-beer !

(*Curtain falls.*)

The Music-hall   Screaming Farcical Comedy.

A Melodrama at the " Surrey "   A pathetic " Comedy-
                                              Drama."

Another

The Opera

A patriotic Drama at the
"National Theatre"

And

Three acts   of Henrik Ibsen

The deplorable issue

"BISHOPS," said the Rev. Mr. Phillips to the Playgoers' Club, "are not really so stiff and starchy as they are made out to be. There is a good heart beneath the gaiters." Calf-love, we presume.

DIFFERENT VIEWS.—Bishops complain of a dearth of candidates for orders. Managers of theatres think differently.

LEG-ITIMATE SUCCESSES.—Modern extrava-ganzas.

THEATRICAL.—The only people who never suffer in the long run—managers of theatres.

"STANDING ORDERS."—Free admissions who can't get seats.

"MOST MUSICAL, MOST MELANCHOLY"

Husband (after the Adagio, to musical wife). "My dear, are
we going to stay to the 'bitter end'?"

MUSIC OF THE FUTURE. SENSATION OPERA. *(See opposite page.)*

AT A PROBLEM PLAY. — *Mr. Dinkershein (eminent critic).* How did you enjoy the piece, Miss MacGuider?

Miss MacGuider. Well, to tell the truth, I didn't know what it was all about.

Mr. Dinkershein. Excellent. The author gives us so much to think of.

QUESTION AND ANSWER.—" Why don't I write plays?" Why should I?

NOT EXACTLY A THEATRICAL MANAGER'S GUIDING MOTTO.—" Piece at any price."

MUSIC OF THE FUTURE. SENSATION OPERA

Manager (to his Primo Tenore, triumphantly). " My dear fellow, I've brought you the score of the new opera. We've arranged *such* a scena for you in the third act! o' board of the Pirate Screw, after the keelhauling scene, you know! Heavy rolling sea, eh?—Yes, and we can have some real spray pumped on to you from the fire-engine! Volumes of smoke from the funnel, close behind your head—in fact, you'll be enveloped as you rush on to the bridge! And then you'll sing that lovely barcarolle through the speaking-trumpet! And mind you hold tight, as the ship blows up just as you come upon your high D in the last bar!!!"

OUR SHAKSPEARIAN SOCIETY.—In the course of a discussion, Mrs. —— observed, that she was positive that Shakspeare was a butcher by trade, because an old uncle of hers had bought *lambs' tails from Shakspeare.*

" SOUND DUES."—Fees to opera box-keepers.

COPYRIGHT AND COPYWRONG.—The dramatist who dramatises his neighbour's novel against his will, is less a playwright than a plagiary.

"CROSS OLD THING!"—*Wife.* "I'm going into town now, dear. Shall I book places for *Caste* or *Much ado about Nothing?*" *Husband.* "Oh, please yourself, my dear; but I should say we've enough 'Ado about Nothing' at home!"

Our Theatricals.—*Brown (rehearsing his part as the "Vicomte de Cherisac").* "Yas, Marie! I've fondly loved ye. *(Sobs dramatically.)* 'Tis well—but no mat-tar-r!" *Housemaid (to cook, outside the door).* "Lauks, 'Liz'beth, ain't master a givin' it to missis!"

TECHNICAL.—*First Player* ("*Juvenile Lead*"). "Play Scene—Hamlet. (*Deferentially*). What do you think of it?" "How precious well them supers a're painted, ain't they?"
Second Player ("*First Heavy*").

A DOUBLE DISAPPOINTMENT.—*Stern Hostess (who is giving private theatricals).* "You are very late, Mr. Fitz Smythe. They've begun long ago!" *Languid Person of Importance (who abominates that particular form of entertainment).* "What! You don't mean to say they're at it still!"

MODEST APPEAL.—*Lady (to big drum),* "Pray, my good man, don't make that horrid noise! I can't hear myself speak!"

53

A MODERN REHEARSAL

Leading Lady (*to Stage Manager*). Who's that man in the ulster coat talking to the call boy?

Stage Manager. Don't know, I'm sure. Perhaps a gas-fitter. Now, as I was saying, Miss Frisette, I think that all your alterations in the dialogue are quite up to date, but we must give Splitter a chance for his cackle. Ah! here he is.

Splitter. Well, old boy, I've worked in that scene to rights, but the boss thinks that some allusions to Turkey served up with German sausage would fetch 'em. So you might chuck it in for me.

Stage Man. Of course I will. Capital idea. (*Marks prompt-book.*) I wonder who that chap is in the wing?

Splitter. Haven't the faintest idea. Looks like an undertaker. Hallo, Wobbler, brought your new song?

Wobbler. Yes, it ought to go. And I've a gross or so of capital wheezes.

54

Younger Son of Ducal House. "Mother, allow me to introduce to you—my wife."
His Wife (late of the Frivolity Theatre). "How do, Duchess? I'm the latest thing in mésalliances !"

Splitter. No poaching, old chap.

Wobbler. Of course not. I'll not let them off when you're on. Morning, Miss Skid. Perfect, I suppose?

Miss Skid (*brightly*). I'm always "perfect." But—(*seriously*)—I had to cut all the idiotic stuff in my part, and get Peter Quip of "The Kangaroo" to put in something up to date. Here's the boss!

[*Enter Mr. Footlyte, the manager, amid a chorus of salutations.*]

Stage Man. Places, ladies and gentlemen.

Mr. Footlyte. Before we begin the rehearsal, I would point out that I have completely rewritten the second act, and——

The Stranger in the Ulster. But, sir, I beg of you to remember——

Mr. F. Who is that man?

Everybody. We don't know!

Mr. F. (*advancing*). Who are you, sir, who dare to trespass on my premises?

The S. in the U. Don't you remember me, Mr. Footlyte?

Mr. F. No, sir, I do not. What's your business?

56

The S. in the U. (*nervously*).   I am the author of the piece.

Everybody.   Ha! ha! ha!

Mr. F.   Then you're not wanted here.   (*To stage manager.*)   Jenkins, clear the stage.

[*The author is shown out.   Rehearsal proceeds. Curtain.*]

MEANT AS A COMPLIMENT.—*Shakspeare Smith* (*to Miss Lagushe, after production of his new comedy*).   And what did you think of my little piece the other night?

Miss Lagushe.   I didn't pay the least attention to the play.   All I thought was, what a cruel ordeal the performance must be for *you!*

NEO-DRAMATIC NURSERY RHYME

MRS. GRUNDY, good woman, scarce knew what to think
About the relation 'twixt drama and drink.
Well, give hall—and theatre—good wholesome diet,
And all who attend will be sober and quiet!

HINTS TO AMATEUR PLAY-WRIGHTS

Of the Essence of Drama.—It is not strictly necessary that you should know much about this, but as a rough indication it may be stated that whenever two or more persons stand (or sit) upon a platform and talk, and other persons, whether from motives of *ennui*, or charity, or malice, or for copyright purposes only, go and listen to them, the law says it is a stage-play. It does not follow that anybody else will.

Of the Divers Sorts of Dramatic Writing.— Owing to the competition nowadays of the variety entertainment you will do well to treat these as practically amalgamated. For example, start Act I. with an entirely farcical and impossible marriage, consequent upon a mistake similar to that of "Mr. Pickwick" about the exact locality of his room ; drop into poetry and pathos in Act II. (waltz-music "off" throughout will show that it *is* poetry and pathos) ; introduce for the first time in Act III. a melodramatic villain, who endeavours to

58

elope with the heroine (already married, as above, and preternaturally conscious of it), and wind-up Act IV. with a skirt dance and a general display of high spirits, with which the audience, seeing that the conclusion is at hand, will probably sympathise. Another mixture, very popular with serious people, may be manufactured by raising the curtain to a hymn tune upon a number of obviously early Christians, and, after thus edifying your audience, cheering them up again with glimpses of attractive young ladies dressed (to a moderate extent) as pagans, and continually in fits of laughter. The performance of this kind of composition is usually accompanied by earthquakes, thunder and lightning ; but the stage carpenter will attend to these.

Of Humour.—Much may be accomplished in this line by giving your characters names that are easily punned upon. Do not forget, however, that even higher flights of wit than you can attain by this means will be surpassed by the simple expedient of withdrawing a chair from behind a gentleman about to sit down upon it. And this only requires a stage-direction.

Of Dialogue.—Speeches of more than half a page,

though useful for clearing up obscurities, are generally deficient in the qualities of repartee. After exclaiming, "Oh, I am slain!" or words to that effect, no character should be given a soliloquy taking more than five minutes in recitation.

Of the Censorship.—This need not be feared unless you are unduly serious. Lady Godiva, for instance, will be all right for a ball where the dress is left to the fancy, but you must not envelop her in problems.

MOTTO FOR THE STAGE-WORSHIPPERS.— "Mummer's the word!"

QUITE OF HER OPINION

Gushing Young Woman (to famous actor). "Oh, do you know, Mr.
Starleigh, I'm simply *mad* to go on the stage!"   *Famous Actor.*
"Yes, I should think you *would* be, my dear young lady!"

61

THE DECLINE OF THE DRAMA

MUNDUNGUS deems the drama is declining,
  Yet fain would swell the crowded playwright ranks.
The secret of his pessimist opining,
  Is—all *his* dramas *are* declined—with thanks!

CONTRIBUTION TOWARDS NURSERY RHYMES

*(For Use of Infant Students in New School of Dramatic
Art)*

'TIS the voice of the prompter,
  I hear him quite plain;
He has prompted me twice,
  Let him prompt me again.

A suggestion to the refreshment departments of our theatres, much simpler than the old method of struggling by, and would prevent the men going out between the acts.

First night of musical comedy.   The authors called before the curtain.

Jones (arriving in the middle of the overture to "Tristan und Isolde"—quite audibly).   "Well, thank goodness we're in *plenty of time !*"

IN THE STALLS

Time past—Crinoline era

APPROPRIATE SHAKSPEARIAN MOTTO FOR A
FIRM OF ADVERTISING AGENTS.—"Posters of
the sea and land."

QUID PRO QUO.—*Actor-Manager* (*to Dramatic
Author*). What I want is a one-part piece.

Dramatic Author. That's very easily arranged.
You be number one. and "part" to me.

IN THE STALLS

Time present—Fan development

Araminta. Why, dearest, do you call those witticisms, which the comedians deliver with such ready humour, "gags"?

Corydon (*the playwright*).   Because they always stifle the author.

[*Smiles no more during the evening.*

THE MUMMER'S BÊTE-NOIR.—"*Benefits* forgot."

MITIGATING CIRCUMSTANCES

Sangazur, Senior. "Look here, what's all this nonsense I hear about your wanting to marry an actress?"

Sangazur, Junior. "It's quite true, sir. But—er—you can have no conception how *very poorly* she acts!"

66

A STUDIED INSULT.—*Box-Office Keeper at the Imperial Music-Hall (to Farmer Murphy, who is in town for the Islington Horse Show).* "Box or two stalls, sir?" *Murphy.* "What the dev'l d'ye mane? D'ye take me an' the missus for a pair o' proize 'osses? Oi'll have two sates in the dhress circle, and let 'em be as dhressy as possible, moind!"

"The Sleeping Beauty."—"Nervous? oh dear no! I only acted *once* in private theatricals, Mr. Jones, and, although it was an important part, I had nothing to say!" "Really? What *was* the part?" "*Can't you guess?*"

68

COLLABORATEURS.—Jennings and Bellamy, the famous dramatists, planning one of those thrilling plays of plot and passion, in which (as everybody knows) Jennings provides the inimitable broad humour, and Bellamy the love-scenes and the tragic deaths. (Bellamy is the shorter of the two.)

WHY I DON'T WRITE PLAYS

(From the Common-place Book of a Novelist)

BECAUSE it is so much pleasanter to read one's work than to hear it on the stage.

Because publishers are far more amiable to deal with than actor-managers.

Because "behind the scenes" is such a disappointing place—except in novels.

Because why waste three weeks on writing a play, when it takes only three years to compose a novel?

Because critics who send articles to magazines inviting one to contribute to the stage, have no right to dictate to us.

Because a fairly successful novel means five hundred pounds, and a fairly successful play yields as many thousands—why be influenced by mercenary motives?

Because all novelists hire their pens in advance for years, and have no time left for outside labour.

And last, and (perhaps) not least, Why don't I send in a play? Because I *have* tried to write *one*, and find I can't quite manage it!

HER FIRST PLAY.—*Mamma* (*who has taken Miss Effie, as a great treat, to a morning performance*). "Hush, dear! You mustn't talk!"
Miss Effie (*with clear sense of injustice, and pointing to the stage*).
"But, mummy,—*they're* talking!"

Q. When are the affairs of a theatre likely to assume a somewhat fishy aspect? *A.* When there's a sole lessee.

Evangeline. Why is this called the dress circle mamma?

Mamma. Because the stalls are the undressed circle, dear.

A Form of Equestrian Drama.—Horseplay.

Mellow drammer

FIRST NIGHT OF AN UNAPPRECIATED MELODRAMA.—*He.* "Are
we alone?" *Voice from the Gallery.* "No, guv'nor; but you will
be to-morrow night."

73

THE COMMISSARIAT

Our Bandmaster (to purveyor of refreshments). "We must hev beef sangwitches, marm! Them ham ones make the men's lips that greasy, they can't blow!"

A NOTE AND QUERY

Wife (*given to literature and the drama*). "George, what is the meaning of the expression, 'Go to!' you meet with so often in Shakspeare and the old dramatists?"

Husband (*not a reading man*). "'Don't know, I'm sure, dear, unless——Well,—p'raps he was going to say——but thought it wouldn't sound proper!"

MR. PUNCH'S OPERA BOX

SIC VOS NON VOBIS DRAMATISATIS, WRITERS!

Wife of his Bosom (just home from the play). "And then that *darling* Walter Lisson, looking like a Greek god, drew his stiletto, and delivered, oh! *such* an exquisite soliloquy over her tomb—all in blank verse—like heavenly music on the organ!"

He. "Why, he's got a voice like a raven, and can no more deliver blank verse than he can fly."

She. "Ah, well—it was very beautiful, all the same—all about love and death, you know!"

He. "Who wrote the piece, then?"

She. "Who wrote the piece? Oh — er — well — his name's sure to be on the bill somewhere — at least I *suppose* it is!"

SIC VOS NON VOBIS DRAMATISATIS,
WRITERS! (*See opposite page.*)

FROM OUR GENERAL THEATRICAL FUND.—
Why would a good-natured dramatic critic be a
valuable specimen in an anatomical museum?
Because he takes to pieces easily.

MEM. BY A MANAGER

To say " boo" to a goose requires some doing.
In theatres 'tis the goose who does the " booing,"
And though a man may do the best he can, sir,
Anser will hiss, though hissing may not answer!

REVISED VERSION OF SHAKSPEARE

    " A POOR player,
Who struts and frets his hour on the stage,
And then—goes in society."

A solo on the horn

AFTER THE PERFORMANCE.—*Rupert the Reckless (Tompkins, a distinguished amateur from town).* " Now, I call it a beastly shame, Jenkins; you haven't ordered that brute of yours off my togs, and you know I can't go back to the inn like *this*

SCENES FROM MR. PUNCH'S PANTOMIME.   Scene I.—The Tragic Mews

SCENES FROM MR. PUNCH'S PANTOMIME. Scene II.—The Comic Mews

AMBIGUOUS.—*First Actress.* "Oh, my dear, I'm feeling so chippy! I think I shall send down a doctor's certificate to-night, to say I can't act." *Second Ditto.* "Surely a certificate isn't necessary, dear?"

Tenor (at amateur concert). "It's my turn next, and I'm so nervous I should like to run away. Would you mind accompanying me, Miss Brown?"

Mrs. Smith. "This is a very unpleasant piece, don't you think? There's certainly a great deal to be done yet in the way of elevating the stage." *Mrs. Jones (who hasn't been able to get a glimpse of the stage all the afternoon).* "Well—er—it would come to much the same thing if you ladies were to lower your hats!"

OUR THEATRICALS.—*The Countess.* "Will this cruel war *never* end? Day after day I watch and wait, straining every nerve to catch the sound of the trumpet that will tell me of my warrior's return. But, hark! what is that I hear?"

[Stage direction.—"*Trumpet faintly heard in distance.*" *But we hadn't rehearsed that, and didn't explain the situation quite clearly to the local cornet-player who helped us on the night.*]

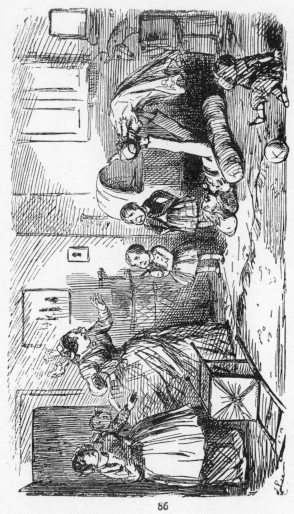

Master Jackey having seen a "professor" of posturing, has a private performance of his own in the nursery.

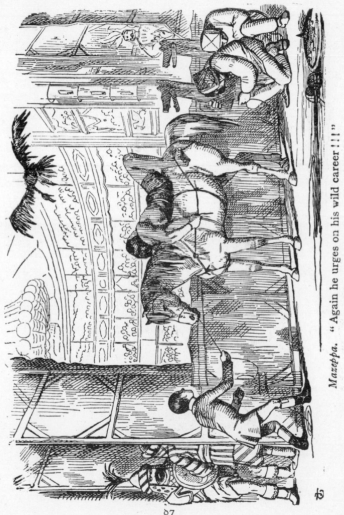

Mazeppa. " Again he urges on his wild career ! ! ! "

DISTINGUISHED AMATEURS. THE ACTOR.—*Billy Wapshot.* "I say, look here, you know! They've cast me for the part of *Sir Guy Earlswoodde,* an awful ass that everyone keeps laughing at! How the dickens am I to act such a beastly part as that?—and how am I to dress for it, I should like to know?" *Brown (stage manager).* "My dear fellow, dress *just as you are!*—and as for acting, *be as natural as you possibly can!* It will be an immense success!"

DISTINGUISHED AMATEURS. THE JEUNE PREMIER. — "*What*, Eleanor? You know *Sir Lionel Wildrake*, the handsomest, wittiest, most dangerous man in town! He of whom it is said that no woman has ever been known to resist him yet!" "The same, Lilian! But hush! He comes——"

[*Enter Colonel Sir Lionel Wildrake.*

THERE is a blessing on peacemakers—is there one on playwrights?

THE HOME OF THE BRITISH DRAMA.—A French crib.

A COURT THEATRE TICKET.—The order of the garter available only at Windsor as an order for the stalls.

NEW NAME FOR A THEATRE WHERE THE ACTORS ARE MORE OR LESS UNINTELLIGIBLE.— "The Mumbles."

Music by handle.

THE SWING OF THE PENDULUM

"And pray, Duke, what possible objection can you have to my being a suitor for the hand of your daughter Gwendolen? I—a—*think* I may flatter myself that, as a leading gentleman at the Parthenon Theatre, my social position is at least on a par with your Grace's!"

"I admit that to be the case just *at present*—but the social position of an actor may suffer a reaction, and a day *may* come when even the leading gentleman at the Parthenon may sink to the level of a *Bishop*, let us say, and be no longer quite a suitable match for a daughter of the —a—House of Beaumanoir!"

TURNING A PHRASE. — *Dramatic Author.* "What the deuce do you mean by pitching into my piece in this brutal manner? It's shameful!" *Dramatic Critic.* "Pitching into it? No, no, no, dear old man—you'll see how pleased I was, *if you'll only read between the lines!*"

SCENE—*A Booth in the Wild West*

The curtain has just fallen on the first act of the " Pirates of the Pacific."

Author. " What is the audience shouting for ? "

Manager. " They're calling for the author."

Author. " Then hadn't I better appear ? "

Manager. " I guess not.   They've got their revolvers in their hands ! "

93

"MEN WERE DECEIVERS EVER"

First Counter Tenor. "Scritchy, I think your wife's waiting for you at our entrance."
Second Counter Tenor. "Oh, then, let's go out at the bass door!"

THE COMMENTATORS.—*First Quidnunc (in an ecstasy).* "I've just been writing to the 'New Shakspeare Society.' 'Believe I've made a discovery—that *Horatio* was *Hamlet's* father!" *Second Quidnunc (enchanted).* "You don't say so!" *First Quidnunc.* "My dear sir, doesn't *Hamlet,* when he handles *Yorick's* skull, address *Horatio,* 'And smelt so, pa'? I think that's conclusive!!"

A DISENCHANTMENT

Very Unsophisticated Old Lady (from the extremely remote country). "*Dear* me! He's a *very* different-looking person from what I had always imagined!"

"JUST HINT A FAULT"

Little Tommy Bodkin takes his cousins to the gallery of the Opera

Pretty Jemima (who is always so considerate). " Tom, dear, don't you think you had better take off your hat, on account of the poor people behind, you know ? "

THE MOAN OF A THEATRE-MANAGER

Who gets, by hook or crook, from me
Admittance free, though well knows he
That myriads turned away will be ?
        The Deadhead.

Who, while he for his programme pays
The smallest silver coin, inveighs
Against such fraud with eyes ablaze ?
        The Deadhead.

Who to his neighbour spins harangues,
On how he views with grievous pangs
The dust that on our hangings hangs ?
        The Deadhead.

Who, in a voice which rings afar,
Declares, while standing at the bar,
Our drinks most deleterious are ?
        The Deadhead.

Who, aye withholds the claps and cheers
That others give ?   Who jeers and sneers
At all he sees and all he hears ?
        The Deadhead.

Who loudly, as the drama's plot
Unfolds, declares the tale a lot
Of balderdash and tommy-rot ?
        The Deadhead.

IBSEN IN BRIXTON.—*Mrs. Harris.* "Yes, William, I've thought
a deal about it, and I find I'm nothing but your doll and dickey-bird,
and so I'm going !"

G 2

Mr. Punch at the Play

Who dubs the actors boorish hinds?
Who fault with all the scenery finds?
Who with disgust his molars grinds?
       The Deadhead.

Who spreads dissatisfaction wide
'Mongst those who else with all they spied
Had been extremely satisfied?
       The Deadhead.

Who runs us down for many a day,
And keeps no end of folks away
That else would for admittance pay?
       The Deadhead.

Who keeps his reputation still,
For recompensing good with ill
With more than pandemonium's skill?
       The Deadhead.

Who makes the bankrupt's doleful doom
In all its blackness o'er me loom?
Who'll bring my grey head to the tomb?
       The Deadhead.

A five bar rest

Seedy Provincial Actor. " Young man, I hear that you propose to essay the *rôle* of the melancholy Dane. What induced you to do it ? " *Prosperous London ditto.* " Oh, I don't know. They egged me on to it." *Seedy Provincial Actor.* " H'm. They egged *me OFF* ! "

LESSONS LEARNED AT A PANTOMIME

(By an Intelligent Schoolboy)

THAT demons are much given to making bad puns, and have on their visiting lists the most beautiful of the fairies.

That the attendants upon the demons (presumably their victims) spend much of their time in break-downs.

That the chief amusement in Fairyland is to stand upon one toe for a distressingly long time.

That the fairies, when they speak, don't seem to have more H.'s to their tongues, than clothes to their backs.

That the fairies have particularly fair complexions, considering they dance so much in the sunlight.

That the tight and scanty costume of the fairies is most insufficient protection from the showers that must be required to produce the gigantic and highly-coloured fairy *flora*.

That the chief fairy (to judge from her allusions to current events) must take in the daily papers.

That harlequin is always shaking his bat, but

THE NEW PLAY

Low Comedian. "Have you seen the notice?"
Tragedian. "No; is it a good one?"
Low Comedian. "It's a fortnight's."

nothing seems to come of it, and that it is hard to say why he comes on or goes off, or, in short, what he's at altogether.

That if clown and pantaloon want to catch columbine, it is hard to see why they don't catch her.

That pantaloon must have been greatly neglected by his children to be exposed without some filial protection to such ill-usage from clown.

That clown leads a reckless and abandoned life, between thefts, butter-slides, hot pokers, nurse-maids, and murdered babies, and on the whole is lucky to escape hanging.

That policemen are made to be chaffed, cuffed, chased, and knocked head-over-heels.

A quick movement with an obligato accompaniment

TERRIFIC SITUATION!

Heroine of domestic drama pursued by the unprincipled villain is about to cast herself headlong from a tremendous precipice!

APPRECIATIVE!

The eldest Miss Bluestocken (to Mrs. Mugby, of the village laundry). I'm delighted that you were able to come to our schoolroom performance of *Scenes from Shakspeare.*

Mrs. Mugby. Oh, so was I, mum. That there "'Amblet"—and the grand lady, mum——

Eldest Miss B. (condescendingly). You mean "Hamlet" and his mother—the vicar and myself. You enjoyed it?

Mrs. Mugby. Oh, we did, mum! We ain't 'ad such a rale good laugh for many a long day.

[*Exit* Miss B., *thinking that Shakspeare is perhaps somewhat thrown away on this yokality.*]

THE BOOK OF THE PLAY (*as managers like it*).— "All places taken for the next fortnight."

WHEN actors complain that all they require is "parts," they generally tell the exact truth.

SCENE FROM SHAKSPEARIAN PANTOMIME

"Where got'st thou that goose?—look!"

(*Macbeth*, Act V., Sc. 3.)

A DISENCHANTMENT.—*Grandpapa.* "*What?* Bob in love with Miss Fontalba, the comic actress at the Parthenon?" *Bob (firing up).* "Yes, grandpa! And if you've got a word to say against that lady, it had better not be said in my presence, that's all!" *Grandpapa.* "I say a word *against* her! Why, bless your heart, my dear boy! I was head over ears in love with her *mysel*—*when I was your age!*"

THE PROBLEM PLAY.—*New Woman* (*with the hat*). "No! My principle is simply *this*—if there's a *demand* for these plays, it must be *supplied!*" *Woman not New* (*with the bonnet*). "Precisely! Just as with the

[*Scorrs*

CHURCH THEATRES FOR COUNTRY VILLAGES—THE BLAMELESS BALLET

["*Mr. Chamberlain has expressed himself in sympathy with the scheme of the Rev. Forbes Phillips for running theatres in connection with the churches in country villages.*"]

There would, our artist imagines, be no difficulty in obtaining willing coryphées among the pew-openers and philanthropic spinsters of the various parishes.

Mr. M'Chrustie (in the washing-room of the Minerva C'ub). "Look here, waiter, what's the meaning of this? These brushes are as beastly grimy as if they'd been blacking boots——!" *Waiter.* "Yes, sir; it's them members from the 'Junior Theshpian,' sir—as are 'ere now, sir. They do dye theirselves to that degree——!"

[Mr. M'C. rushes off and writes furiously to the Committee!

Q. WHAT were the "palmy" days of the drama?

A. When they were first-rate hands at acting.

MOTTO FOR ALL DRAMATIC PERFORMERS.— "Act well your part."

A BAND-BOX.—An orchestra.

"WHAT an awful voice that man's got!" said the manager, who was listening to the throaty tenor.

"Call that **a** voice," said his friend; "it's a disease!"

A PRIVATE BOX.—A sentry box.

"You can't sit there, mum. These here seats are reserved."
"You don't seem to be aware that I'm one of the directors' wives!"
"And if you was his *only* wife, mum, I couldn't let you sit here."

DURING the dull season a certain manager has issued such a number of his autographs in order to ensure the proper filling of his house that he has in playfulness conferred on it the nickname of the ordertorium.

WHAT MANAGERS, ACTRESSES, AND SPECTATORS ALL WANT.—A good dressing.

CHRISTMAS MUSIC FOR THEATRES. — The "waits ' between the acts.

WHAT we want for the British drama generally is not so much native talent as imagi-native talent.

AT THE MUSIC HALLS.—The birds that fly by night—the acro-bats.

CONFRÈRES.—*Master Jacky (who took part in some school theatricals last term,—suddenly, to eminent tragedian who has come to call).* "I say, you know—I act!"

H 2

A PROP OF THE DRAMA

" What, back already, Archie! Was it a dull piece, then ? "

" Don't know. Didn't stop to see. Just looked round stalls and boxes, and didn't see a soul I knew !—so I came away."

SHOWING THAT SOMETIMES IT IS GOOD FOR A COBBLER *NOT* TO STICK TO HIS LAST

Fair Matron. "I remember your acting ' *Sir Anthony*,' *years* ago, when I was a girl, Sir Charles! You did it splendidly!"

The Great Mathematician. "Ah, would you believe it, that bit of acting brought me more compliments than anything I ever did?"

Fair Matron. "I should *think* so, indeed!"

THE COMPANY THAT FREQUENTLY FILLS A
THEATRE BETTER THAN A DRAMATIC ONE.—
The Stationers' Company.

THE managers of Drury Lane, Gaiety, Alhambra
and Empire Theatres ought *ex-officio* to be members of the Worshipful Guild of Spectacle-makers.

"*Walking Lady*" (*late for rehearsal*).   "Oh. I'm *so* sorry to be late!
I *do* hope you haven't all been waiting for me?"
    Stage Manager (*icily*).   "My dear Miss Chalmers, incompetence
is the gift of heaven; but attention to business may be cultivated!"

An Unkind Cut.—*Amateur.* "It was very kind of you to come to our performance the other night; but what did you think of my *Hamlet?* Pretty good?" *Professional (feigning ecstasy).* "Oh, my dear fellow, 'pon my word you know,—really I assure you, good's not the word!"

First Critic. "Well, have you seen the great tragedian in *Romeo and Juliet?*"
Second ditto. "I have; and I confess he didn't come up to my ixpictations. To tell ye the truth, I niver thought he would!"

A CROWDED HOUSE

Angry Voice (from a back seat). "Ears off in front there, please!"

THE PROVINCIAL DRAMA

The Marquis (*in the play*).   "Aven't I give' yer the edgication of a gen'leman?"

Lord Adolphus (*spendthrift heir*).   "You 'ave!!"

A CONDUCTOR OF HEAT

"STARTLING EFFECTS!"

Peep-Showman. "On the right you observe the 'xpress train a-comin' along, an' the signal lights, the green and the red. The green lights means 'caution,' and the red lights si'nifies 'danger'"——

Small Boy (with his eye to the aperture). "But what's the yaller light, sir?"

Peep-Showman (slow and impressive). "There ain't no yaller light—but the green and the red. The green lights means 'caution,' and the red lights si'nif——"

Small Boy (persistently). "But wha's the other light, sir?"

Peep-Showman (losing patience). "Tell yer there ain't no"——*(takes a look—in consternation)*—"Blowed if the darned old show ain't a-fire!!"

"STARTLING EFFECTS!" (*See opposite page.*)

EX NIHILO NIHIL FIT

["Fashions in drama change as frequently as fashions in hats. It has been reserved for our own day to evolve the comedy of nothing-in-particular. Nowadays nothing happens in a play."—*The Outlook.*]

SCENE—*Nowhere in particular.*

CHARACTERS.

HE, *a nonentity.*

SHE, *another.*

He. Dear—— !

She (*wearily*).   Oh please don't.

[*Does nothing.*

He. Why, what's the matter?

She. Nothing.   [*He aoes nothing.*

She. Well, you may as well go on.   It will be something, anyhow.   (*Yawns.*)   Nothing ever seems to happen in this play.   I don't know why.   It isn't my fault.   Oh, go on.

He. All right.   Don't suppose it amuses me, though.   Darling, I love you—will you marry me?

She (*very wearily*).   Oh, I suppose so.

He.   Thanks very much.   (*Kisses her.*)   There!

[*Returns proudly to his seat, and does nothing.*

126

HOW HE OUGHT *NOT* TO LOOK

*Excited Prompter (to the Ghost of Hamlet's father, who is
working himself up to the most funereal aspect he can assume).*
" Now then, Walker, *LOOK ALIVE !* "

She (with sudden excitement). Supposing I had said " No," would you have shot yourself?—would you have gone to the front?—would your life have been a blank hereafter? Would anything interesting have happened?

He (with a great determination in his eyes). Had you spurned my love——

She (excitedly). Yes, yes?

He (with emotion).—I should have—I should have—done nothing.   [*Does it.*

She. Oh!

He. Yes. As for shooting or drowning myself if any little thing of that sort had happened it would have been *off* the stage. I hope I know my place.   [*She does nothing.*

He (politely). I don't know if you're keen about stopping here? If not, we might——

She. We must wait till somebody else comes on.

He. True. (*Reflects deeply.*) Er—do you mote much?

[*She sleeps. The audience follows suit.*
Curtain eventually.

PREHISTORIC SHAKSPEARE.—" MACBETH "

" Infirm of purpose !
Give me the daggers."—*Act II., Sc.* 2.

MUSIC-HALL INANITIES.—I.

*Miss Birdie Vandeleur (" Society's Pet "—vide her advertisements
passim) bawls the refrain of her latest song :—*

"Ow, I am sow orferly *shy*, boys!
I am, and I kennot tell wy, boys!
  Some dy, wen I'm owlder,
  Per'aps I'll git bowlder,
But naow I am **orfer**-ly shy!"

'E's not a *tall* man—   Nor a *short* man—   But he's just the man for me,'

" Not in the army—   Nor the nivy—   But the royal artill-er-ee !

MUSIC-HALL INANITIES.—II. The Illustrative Method

ATTENTION AT THE PLAY

(*As performed at many London Theatres*)

SCENE—*Interior of a Private Box.*

TIME—*Towards the end of the First Act of an established success.*

PRESENT—*A party of Four.*

No. 1 (*gazing through opera glasses*). A good house. Do you know anyone?

No. 2. Not a soul. Stay—aren't those the Fitzsnooks?

No. 3 (*also using a magnifier*). You mean the woman in the red feather at the end of the third row of the stalls?

No. 4. You have spotted them. They have got Bobby Tenterfore with them. You know, the Johnnie in the F. O.

No. 1. I thought Mr. Tenterfore was at Vienna.

No. 4. No; he *was* going, but they sent another chap. Brought him back from somewhere in the tropics.

MELODRAMA IN THE SUBURBS.—*Elder Sister.* "Do give up, Nellie! They're only acting."
Nellie (tearfully). "You leave me alone. I'm enjoying it!"

No. 3. Then what is Mr. Tenterfore doing in town ?

No. 4. Oh ! come home on leave. Lots of that sort of thing at the F. O.

No. 1 (*having grown weary of looking at the audience*). By the way, *à propos de bottes*, I have some money to invest. Can you suggest anything ?

No. 3. They say that Diddlers Deferred will turn up trumps.

No. 1. What do you mean by that ? I only want to pop in and out between the accounts.

No. 3. Then the Diddlers ought to suit you. They rose six last week, and ought to touch ten before settling day.

No. 1. Then I am on. Thanks very much for the information. Ah ! the curtain has fallen. So much for the first act ! (*Enter visitor.*) Ah ! how are you ? Where are you ?

Visitor. Well, I have got a stall, but I have only just come into the house. What are they playing ?

No. 2. I am sure I don't know ; but if you are curious about it, here's the programme.

Visitor. And what's it all about ?

THE RULING PASSION.—*Doctor.* "No, my dear sir, we must keep ourselves quiet for the present. No stimulants—nothing more exciting than gruel. Gruel for breakfast, gruel for luncheon, gruel for dinner, gruel for——," *Peter Pundoleful (a noted burlesque writer—though you wouldn't have thought it to look at him—rousing himself suddenly).* "Ah! my dear doctor, why is there not a society for the prevention of gruelty to animals?"

No. 1 (*on behalf of self and companions*). We haven't the faintest notion.

> [*Conversation becomes general, and remains so until the end of the evening, regardless of the dialogue on the stage side of the curtain.*

HIS FIRST AND LAST PLAY

RALPH ESSENDEAN, *aged about fifty, is discovered at a writing-desk. He studies a newspaper, from which he reads aloud, thoughtfully:—" So that a successful play may bring its author anything from five to twenty thousand pounds." He lays down the paper, mutters, " H'm !" and taking up a pencil bites it meditatively. Enter Mrs. Essendean.*

Mrs. Essendean (*crossing to Ralph, and placing her hand on his shoulder, asks affectionately*). Well, dear, and how is the play getting on ?

Ralph (*irritably*). You talk of the play, Matilda, as though it were possible to write a four-act drama in ten minutes. The play is not getting on

PARADOXICAL.—*Ethel.* "It was a most wonderful performance, Aunt Tabitha! First, she was shot out of a cannon's mouth on to a trapeze fifteen yards above the orchestra, and then she swung herself up till she stood on a rope on one leg at least a hundred and twenty feet above our heads!" *Aunt Tabitha.* "Ah! I always think a woman *lowers* herself when she does that!"

at all well, for the simple reason that I am only just thinking out the idea.

Mrs. Essendean (*seating herself by the table*). How nice, dear ! And what *is* the idea ?

Ralph (*grimly*). That is just what I am wondering about. Now if you will kindly retire to the kitchen and make an omelette, or discharge the cook, I shall be obliged. [*Leans over his desk.*

Mrs. E. But, dear, I am sure the cook is a most excellent servant, and——

Ralph (*turning round and speaking with repressed exasperation*). That was simply my attempt at a humorous explanation of my wish to be alone, Matilda.

Mrs. E. (*smiling indulgently and rising*). Well, dear, of course if it's going to be a *funny* play, I know you would like to be alone. (*Pausing at the open door.*) And will you read it to us after dinner ? You know the Willoughby-Smythes will be here, and Mr. and Mrs. Vallance from the Bank are coming in afterwards. I am sure they would like to hear it.

Ralph (*irritably*). The play isn't written yet. (*Plaintively.*) *Do* go !

FORM

First Masher. "Let's stop and look at Punch and Judy, old chappie! I've heard it's as good as a play
Second Masher. "I dessay it is, my brave boy. But we ain't dressed, you know!"

Mrs. E. (*sweetly*). I'm sure you'd like to be alone. Don't keep dinner waiting.

[*Beams on him affectionately and exit. Ralph gives a sigh of relief, rumples his hair, and then writes for a few minutes. Then pauses, leans back, biting his pencil, when the door is flung open, and a very good imitation of a whirlwind bursts into the room. The whirlwind is a robust person of forty, he has a large round red face fringed with sandy whiskers, and is one mass of health and happiness. He wears Norfolk jacket, knickerbockers, gaiters and thick boots, and carries a golfing bag. He slaps Ralph heartily on the back, and laughs boisterously. Ralph collapses.*

Tom (*heartily*). How are you? Going strong— what? Asked the wife for you, and she told me you were in here writing a play. Rippin' idea—what?

Ralph (*worried, but striving to be pleasant and polite*). What do you want, old chap?

Tom (*cheerfully*). Nothin' particular, only just to see how you were gettin' on—what? Do you good to have half an hour out, just a few holes— golf—what?

PROPERTY HAS ITS RIGHTS

SCENE: *Mr. Foote Lyter's back Drawing-room. Private Theatricals. Dress Rehearsal.*

Mr. Foote Lyter. "I say, Drawle, while the Duke is having his scene with Dora, where am I to stand!" *Captain Drawle (amateur stage manager).* "Well—er—my dear fellow—er—it's your own house, you know—you can stand where you like!"

Ralph (*with great self-restraint*). Thanks, old man. Not now. You don't mind my asking you to leave me to myself a bit?

Tom (*amiably rising and picking up his bag*). All right, old chap, you know best—what? Thought I'd just look in—hey?—what? Well, I'm off. (*Goes to door, thinks for a moment, and then turns round.*) I say, I know Thingummy's acting manager. If I can put in a word about your play—hey?—what?

Ralph (*rises hurriedly. Shakes hands with Tom, and skilfully manœuvres him into the passage, then calls after him*). Good-bye, old man, and many thanks. (*Closes the door and returns to his desk, grinding his teeth.*) Confound him! (*Takes up paper and writes a few lines, then reads aloud.*) " Puffington puts the letter in his pocket and passes his hand through his hair. He groans ' O, why did I ever write those letters? I know Flossie, and this means fifty pounds at least, and if ever my mother-in-law gets to hear of it! O, lor here she is ' " (*Puts down the paper and looks up at the ceiling.*) Now, speaking to myself as one man to another, I can't help thinking that this sort of thing has been done before. I seem to have

THE **POINT OF VIEW.**—*Exasperated Old Gentleman* (*to lady in front of him*). "Excuse me, madam, but my seat has cost me ten shillings, and I want to see. Your hat—" *The Lady.* "My hat has cost me ten *guineas*, sir, and I want it to *be seen!*"

143

heard it somewhere. I'll—I'll—try a fresh start. (*Writes hurriedly for a few minutes and then reads.*) "Scene.—Fashionable watering place, the beach is crowded; on the pier the band is playing a dreamy waltz. Edwin and Maud are discovered in an open boat. *Edwin.* You must be tired of rowing, sweetest; come and steer. *Maud.* Just as you like, darling. (*As they change seats the boat capsizes. After clinging for twenty minutes to the upturned keel, they are rescued by a passing steamer.*)" That's all right for a "situation," but there seems a lack of dialogue. They can't very well talk while they are clinging to the boat; and what the deuce could they be talking about before? If I let them drown I shall have to introduce fresh characters. Bother! (*Meditates with frowning brow.*) Playwriting appears to present more difficulties than I thought. (*Takes up a newspaper.*) "May bring in anything from five to twenty thousand pounds!" Sounds tempting, but I wonder how it's done?

[*Takes a cigar from the mantelpiece, lights it, and, seating himself near the fire, smokes thoughtfully. Gradually his head sinks back on to the*

Tomkins, who has recently made his appearance *en amateur* as the Melancholy Dane, goes to have his photograph taken "in character." Unfortunately, on reaching the corner of the street, he finds *the road is up*, and he has to walk to the door! Tableau !!

Clever Juvenile (loq.). "Shakspeare? Pooh! For my part I consider Shakspeare a very much over-rated man."

top of the chair, the cigar drops from his relaxed fingers, and as he sleeps, the shadow of a smile breaks across his face. An hour elapses; he is still sleeping. Enter Mrs. Essendean, who brushes against the writing-table and sweeps the sheets of manuscript to the ground.

Mrs. Essendean (crossing to Ralph and lightly shaking him). My dear, my dear, not dressed yet! Do you know the time—just the half-hour.

THE FORTHCOMING PANTOMIME

Astonished Friend. " Why!—Why! What on earth are these ? "

Manager. "These? Oh! These are *fairies!!*"

MR. PUNCH'S PATENT MATINEE HAT,

Fitted with binocular glasses for the benefit of those sitting
behind its wearer.

(*Ralph starts up.*) Eh? (*Looks at the clock.*)
Nearly half past, by Jove! I shan't be two
seconds. [*Rushes hastily from the room.*

Mrs. Essendean (*picks up the extinguished cigar,
and drops it daintily into the fire. Looks round the*

HEARD AT A PROVINCIAL CIRCUS.—*Wag (to unfortunate small gent, who has vainly endeavoured to persuade lady to remove her hat).* "Don't you see she's got a bird in her hat, sitting? You wouldn't have the lady addle-headed, would you?"

room and sees the littering manuscript.) What an untidy old thing it is! (*Picks up the sheets, crumples them into a ball and throws them into the waste-paper basket.*) There, that looks better.

[*Gazes into the mirror, pats her hair, and exit.*

(*End of the play.*)

THE AMATEURS.—*Suburban Roscius.* "Ah, I saw you were at our 'theatricals' the other night. How did you like my assumption of *Hamlet?*"   *Candid Friend.* "My dear f'llar—great'st piece of assumption I ever saw i' m' life!"

CAUSE AND EFFECT

Eminent Provincial Tragedian. "Come hithorr, sweet one! Your mothorr tells me that you shed teorrs during my soliloquy in exile, last night!"

Sweet One. "Yes, sir. Mother kept on pinching me, 'cause I was so sleepy!"

"EXCLUSIVE"

Our Philanthropist (who often takes the shilling gallery—to his neighbour). "Only a middling house."

Unwashed Artisan. "Ay—that sixpence extry, 'rather heavy for the likes o' huz, y'know. But there's one thing —it keeps out the riff-raff!!"

THE DRAMA.—*Æsthetic Critic* (*at the club, after the theatre*).
"Can you imagine anything more utterly solemn than the
dénoûment in *Romeo and Juliet?* Two lovers, both dying
in the same vault! What fate more weirdly tragic
could——"

Cynical Old Bachelor (*who has evidently never read the
play*). "Um—'s no knowing. The author might 'a'
married 'em!"

Distinguished Amateur (about to make his first appearance in public at a concert for the people). "Oh, I do feel so nervous!" *Sympathetic Friend.* "Oh, there's no occasion to be nervous, my dear fellow. They applaud *anything!*"

THE MAIDEN'S POINT OF VIEW.—Mamma (to Maud, who has been with her brother to the play, and is full of it). "But was there no love in the piece, then?" Maud. "Love? Oh dear no, mamma. The principal characters were husband and wife, you know!"

LA COMEDIE FRANÇAISE

Jones (who understands French so well, although he does not speak it), reading over list of pieces to be played at the Gaiety:—"'Le Gendre de M. Poirier.' Why, what gender *should* the man be, I should like to know!"

"THOSE WHO LIVE IN GLASS HOUSES," ETC.—*The Bishop*. "I hope your grandchildren liked the circus, Lady Godiva. That was a wonderful performance of Mlle. Petitpas on the bare-backed steed, wasn't it?" *Lady Godiva*. "Yes—a—but I dislike those bare-backed performances. They're so risky, you know!"

A very cold audience. (Suggestion for the stalls in mid-winter)

A CASE OF "NO COMPRENNY"

"Ha! Mistare Robinson! 'Ow do you do? 'Av you seen ze last new piece at ze 'Olleborne? Supairrb! Splendeed!! Good!!!"

"A—no—I don't patronise the English drama. I like finish, delicacy, refinement; and I'm happy to say I've secured tickets for all the French plays!"

"Tiens! Mais vous savez le Français, alors?"

"A—I beg your pardon?"

"Je vous demande si vous savez le Français, parbleu! Cruche, Melon, Baudet, Dinde, Jobard, Crétin, Momie, Colin-Maillard que vous êtes?"

"A—quite so! No doubt! A—by the bye, have you seen Jones lately?"

A CASE OF "NO COMPRENNY"

(*See opposite page.*)

BETWEEN THE ACTS ; OR, THE DRAMA IN LIQUOR

SCENE—*Refreshment Saloon at a London Theatre. A three-play bill forms the evening's entertainment. First Act over. Enter Brown, Jones, and Robinson.*

Brown. Well, really a very pleasant little piece. Quite amusing. Yes ; I think I will have a cup of coffee or a glass of lemonade. Too soon after dinner for anything stronger.

Jones. Yes, and really, after laughing so much, one gets a thirst for what they call light refreshments. I will have some gingerbeer.

Robinson. Well, I think I will stick to iced-water. You know the Americans are very fond of that. They always take it at meal-times, and really after that capital *équivoque* one feels quite satisfied. (*They are served by the bar attendant.*) That was really very funny, where he hides behind the door when she is not looking.

[*Laughs at the recollection.*

160

Manager of "Freak" Show. "Have I got a vacancy for a giant? Why, you don't look five feet!" *Candidate.* "Yes, that's just it. I'm the smallest giant on record!"

Brown. And when the uncle sits down upon the band-box and crushes the canary-cage! [*Chuckles.*

Jones. Most clever. But there goes the bell, and the curtain will be up directly. Rather clever, I am told. The *Rose of Rouen*—it is founded on the life of *Joan of Arc.* I am rather fond of these historical studies.

Brown. So am I. They are very interesting.

Robinson. Do you think so? Well, so far as I am concerned, I prefer melodrama. Judging from the title, *The Gory Hand* should be uncommonly good.

[*Exeunt into Theatre. After a pause they return to the Refreshment Room.*

Brown. Well, it is very clever; but I confess it beats me. (*To bar attendant.*) We will all take soda-water. No, thanks, quite neat, and for these gentlemen too.

Jones. Well, I call it a most excellent psychological study. However, wants a clear head to understand it. (*Sips his soda-water.*) I don't see how she can take the flag from the Bishop, and yet want to marry the Englishman.

Robinson. Ah, but that was before the vision.

An Irresistible Appeal.—*Mrs. Blokey (who has called with a letter of introduction on Mr. Roscius Lamborn, the famous actor and manager).* "And I've brought you my son, who's breakin' his mother's 'art, Mr. Lamborn! He insists on givin' up the city and goin' on the stage—and his father an alderman and 'im in his father's business, and all the family thought of so 'ighly in Clapham! It's a *great grief* to us, *I assure* you, Mr. Lamborn! Oh! if you could only dissuade 'im! But it's too late for that, I'm afraid, so p'raps you wouldn't mind givin' him a leadin' part in your next piece!"

If you think it over carefully, you will see it was natural enough. Of course, you must allow for the spirit of the period, and other surrounding circumstances.

Brown. Are you going to stay for *The Gory Hand?*

Jones. Not I. I am tired of play-acting, and think we have had enough of it.

Robinson. Well, I think I shall look in. I am rather fond of strong scenes, and it should be good, to judge from the programme.

Jones. Well, we will "sit out." It's rather gruesome. Quite different from the other plays.

Robinson. Well, I don't mind horrors—in fact, like them. There goes the bell. So I am off. Wait until I come back.

Brown. That depends how long you are away. Ta, ta !   [*Exit Robinson.*

Jones. Now, how a fellow can enjoy a piece like that, I cannot understand. It is full of murders, from the rise to the fall of the curtain.

Brown. Yes—but Robinson likes that sort of thing. You will see by-and-by how the plot will affect him. It is rather jumpy, especially at the

WHAT OUR DRAMATIST HAS TO PUT UP WITH.—*His Wife (reading a Sunday paper)*. "*A propos* of *Hamlet*, they say here that you and Shakspeare represent the very opposite poles of the dramatic art!" *He.* "Ah! that's a nasty one for Shakspeare!"

end, when the severed head tells the story of the murder to the assistant executioner. I would not see it again on any account.

Jones. No—it sent my maiden aunt in hysterics. However, it has the merit of being short. (*Applause.*) Ah, there it's over! Let's see how Robinson likes it. That *tableau* at the end, of the starving-coastguardsman expiring under the rack, is perfectly awful! (*Enter Robinson, staggering in.*) Why, my boy, what's the matter?

Brown. You do look scared! Have something to drink? That will set it all to-rights!

Robinson (*with his eyes protruding from his head, from horror*). Help, help! help! (*After a long shudder.*) Brandy! Brandy!! Brandy!!!

> [*At all the places at the bar there is a general demand for alcohol.*

Brown. Yes. Irving was right; soda-water does very well for Shakspeare's histories, but when you come to a piece like *The Bells*, you require supporting. [*Curtain and moral.*

OVERHEARD OUTSIDE A THEATRE

"Yah! Waitin' ter see der *kids* play!"

Actor (*excitedly*). "For *two* long *years* have I——"
A Voice from above. "So you 'ave, guv'nor!"

STUDY

Of an ancient buck at a modern burlesque

COLOURED CLERGY

(*A Memory of St. James's Hall*)

Uncle (can't see so well as he did, and a little hard of hearing).
" Who do you say they are, my dear !—Christian ministers ?
'Ncom'ly kind of 'em to give a concert, to be sure ! For a
charitable purpose, I 've no doubt, my dear ! ! "

SUPEREROGATION

Country Maid (having first seen "missus" and the children into a cab). "O, coachman, do you know the principal entrance to Drury Lane Theat——?"

Crabbed Old Cabby (with expression of ineffable contempt). "Do I know! Kim aup——!"

Jones (alluding to the song). " Not bad ; but I think the girl might have put a little more *spirit* into it with advantage."

Lushington. " Jush 't I was thinkin.' Lesh avanother!"

172

AFTER THE THEATRICALS.—" What on earth made you tell that appalling little cad that he ought to have trod the boards of ancient Greece! You surely didn't really admire his acting?"   "Oh no! But, you know, the Greek actors used to wear masks!"

"Jemmy! What's a stall at the hopera?"
"Well, I can't say, not for certain; but I suppose it's where they sells the happles, horanges, ginger-beer, and biskits."

" Please, sir! give us your ticket if you aint agoin' in
again."

A DOMESTIC DRAMA

"Admit two to the boxes."

PROGRESS

Young Rustic. "Gran'fa'r, who was Shylock?"
Senior (after a pause). "Lauk a' mussy, bo', yeou goo to Sunday skewl, and don't know that!"

"Oh, that this too, too solid flesh would melt!"— Act I., Sc. 2.

"I could a tail **unfold**" —*Ibid.*

"What a falling off was there!"—*Ibid.*

"Methinks I scent the morning hair!"—*Ibid.*

"Brief let me be!"—*Ibid.*

"Lend thy serious earring to what I shall unfold!"—Act. I., Sc. 5.

"HAMLET" A LA SAUCE DUMB-CRAMBO

"Toby, or not Toby? that is the question."—Act. II., Sc. 2.

"The King, sir."—"Ay, sir, what of him?" "Is in his retirement marvellous distempered." — "With drink, sir!"—"No, my lord, rather with collar!"—Act III., Sc. 2.

"Oh, my offence is rank!"—Act III., Sc. 3.

"Put your bonnet to his right use — 'tis for the head."—Act V., Sc. 2.

"COMING EVENTS CAST THEIR SHADOWS BEFORE THEM."—
Domesticated Wife. "Oh, George, I wish you'd just——" *Talented
Husband (author of various successful comic songs for music halls,
writer of pantomimes and variety-show libretti).* "Oh, for goodness
sake, Lucy, don't bother me *now!* You might *see* I'm trying to work
out some *quite* new lines for the fairy in the transformation scene of
the pantomime!"

A SENSITIVE EAR

Intelligent Briton. "But we have no theatre, no actors worthy of
the name, mademoiselle! Why, the English delivery of blank verse
is simply torture to an ear accustomed to hear it given its full
beauty and significance by a Bernhardt or a Coquelin!"

Mademoiselle. "Indeed? I have never heard Bernhardt or
Coquelin recite English blank verse!"

Intelligent Briton. "Of course not. I mean *French* blank verse—
the blank verse of Corneille, Racine, Molière!"

Mademoiselle. "Oh, monsieur, there is no such thing!"

[Briton still tries to look intelligent.

A SENSITIVE EAR. (*See opposite page.*)

DUMB-CRAMBO'S GUIDE TO THE LONDON THEATRES

Drew wry lane

Cove in garden

Cry-teary 'un

Prints of whales

" A—mark it ! "

Gay at tea

Princesses and royal tea

Globe

"Scent, James?"

Strand and "save, hoi!"

Only in play!

The actor who has his head
turned with applause

CURTAIN-RAISERS

Extract from Ethel's correspondence :—" At the last moment something went wrong with the curtain, and we had to do without one! It was awful! But the Rector explained matters to the front row, and they came to the rescue *nobly !*"

" Well, how did the new play go off last night?"
" Oh, there was a sleep-walking scene in the third act that was
rather effective."   ": A la Lady Macbeth, eh?"
' Well—not exactly.   It was the audience that got up in its sleep
and walked out!"

MUSIC HALL TYPES

I.—The " Lion Comique "

ON TOUR.—*Heavy Tragedian.* " Do you let apartments to—ah—the profession ? " *Unsophisticated Landlady.* " Oh, yes, sir. Why, last week we had the performing dogs here ! "

MUSIC HALL TYPES

II.—The " Serio "

ART AND NATURE. *(Overheard during the Private Theatricals.)*—
She. "How well your wife plays *Lady Geraldine*, Mr. Jones. I think
the way she puts on that awful affected tone is just splendid. How
does she manage it?" *Mr. Jones (with embarrassment).* "Er—
she doesn't. That's her natural voice."

MUSIC HALL TYPES

III.—The " Refined Comedian "